When Riddles Come Rumbling

POEMS to PONDER

by Rebecca Kai Dotlich

Illustrated by
Karen Dugan

WORDSONG

AN IMPRINT OF HIGHLIGHTS

Honesdale, Pennsylvania

For my nephew John, who rumbles through my life.
May poetry always rumble through yours.

—RKD

To everyone at the Plainville Public Library:
Melissa Campbell, director; Stan Kozcera, Georgia Finnegan,
Judith Meixner, Helena Moore, and Terry Murphy.
Many, many thanks.

—KD

Text copyright © 2001 by Rebecca Kai Dotlich
Illustrations copyright © 2001 by Karen Dugan
All rights reserved
For information about permission to reproduce selections from this book,
please contact permissions@highlights.com.

WordSong
An Imprint of Highlights
815 Church Street
Honesdale, Pennsylvania 18431
wordsongpoetry.com
Printed in China

U.S. Cataloging-in-Publication Data
    (Library of Congress Standards)

Dotlich, Rebecca Kai.
    When riddles come rumbling : poems to ponder / by Rebecca Kai Dotlich ;
illustrated by Karen Dugan.— 1st ed.
 [32] p. : col. ill. ; cm.
Summary of Publication: A collection of riddle poems with context clues.
ISBN: 978-1-56397-846-3 (hc) • ISBN: 978-1-62091-031-3 (pb)
1. Riddles — Juvenile poetry. 2. Children's poetry. [1. Riddles.
2. Poetry.] I. Dugan, Karen. II. Title.
811.54 21 2001   CIP
2001086533

First edition, 2001
The text of this book is set in Clearface Regular.

10 9 8 7 6 5 4 3 2 1

Riddle Answers (in page order):

gum ball, roller coaster, hula hoop, yo-yo, kite, chrysalis, trampoline, fireworks, water slide, spider, snake, carrots, soup, snowflakes, marbles, button and buttonhole, pizza, clock, tea, telephone, diary, licorice, braces, crane, *Titanic*, telescope, island, octopus, poet.

When riddles come rumbling
as no doubt they do,
such poems are to ponder
as clue after clue
weaves words
into puzzles
then welcomes you in,
when riddles come rumbling
it's time to
begin . . .

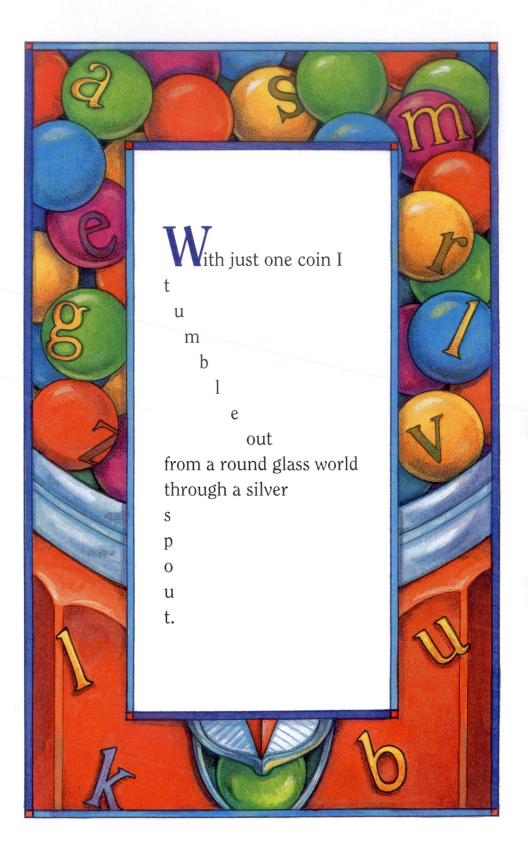

With just one coin I

t

   u

     m

       b

         l

           e

              out

from a round glass world

through a silver

s

p

o

u

t.

I grunt
and grumble
as I go.
Racing,
rumbling,
as I throw
you over,
under,
inside out,
I dash you
         d
            o
               w
                  n
and all about,
I twirl you,
whirl you
like the wind.
I thrill you,
till you
reach
the
e
n
d.

This ring of wonder
spins around—
below the waist,
above the ground,
round and round
the circle flies,
a whirling,
whizzing
hip-surprise,
but if you pause
to shout or cheer,
this twirling,
twisting
summer-sphere
s l i g h t l y
s
   l
      i
        p
           s,   sort of
s t a l l s,
l i m p s
       and h o b b l e s,
finally
f
a
l
l
s.

I rock the cradle,
I swirl
and snap—
I take a swooping
midair lap,
looping all
around your hand,
my dazzling Duncan
tricks are grand—
see me spin
and skim
your feet.
Around the World
is now complete!

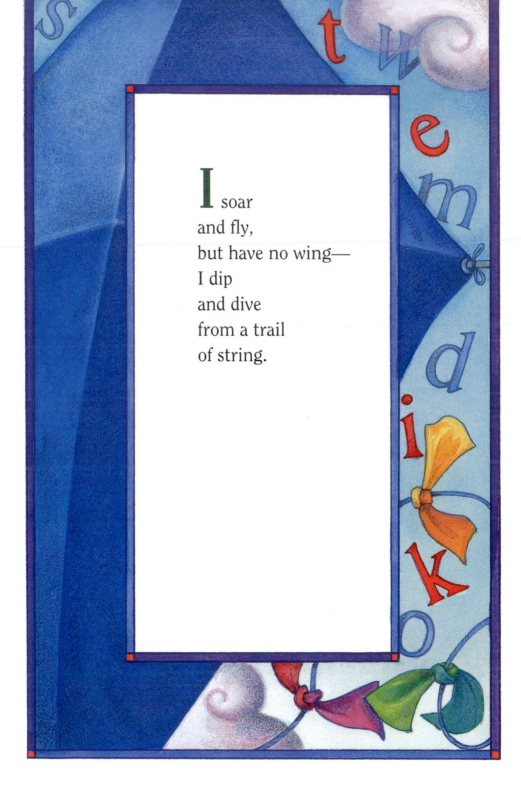

I soar
and fly,
but have no wing—
I dip
and dive
from a trail
of string.

I'm fastened firm
upon this limb,
this brown shell-skin
is warm inside,
a place to hide
until I grow—
the breezes blow
a cradlesong;
it sings to me
of wings
and sky—
it won't be long
before I fly.

I send you flying in the air,
warm wind whistling
through your hair;
you're jumping, jouncing,
all around;
somersaulting,
then
you're down,
bouncing hard
on your behind—
but it's such fun,
you don't
much mind.

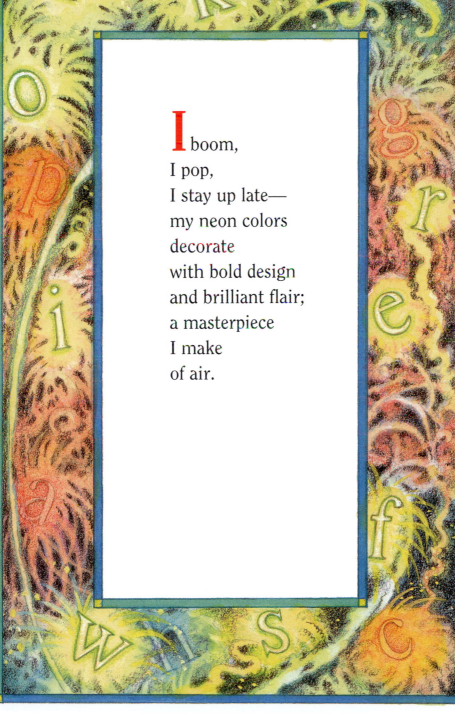

I boom,
I pop,
I stay up late—
my neon colors
decorate
with bold design
and brilliant flair;
a masterpiece
I make
of air.

You climb to reach
the top of me,
then quick as a blink
in a free-falling sea
you sail away
you twist and wind
with a pillow of water
at your behind—
then long and smooth
your body glides
your wet bare feet
propel the ride
as quickly you
go s a i l i n g through
a giant wave
of splashing
blue.

You spin a zillion
silver threads
to weave yourself
a garden bed;
below the stars,
beneath the sun,
cling tight to your quilt,
sweet eight-legged one.

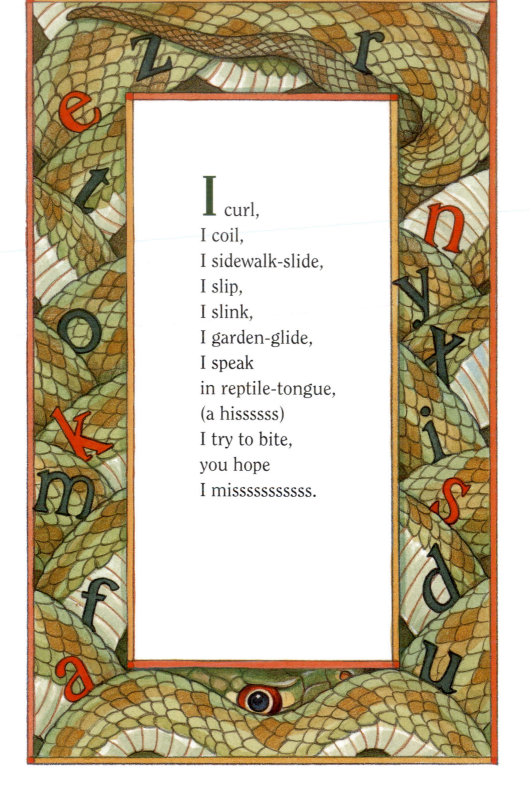

I curl,
I coil,
I sidewalk-slide,
I slip,
I slink,
I garden-glide,
I speak
in reptile-tongue,
(a hissssss)
I try to bite,
you hope
I missssssssssss.

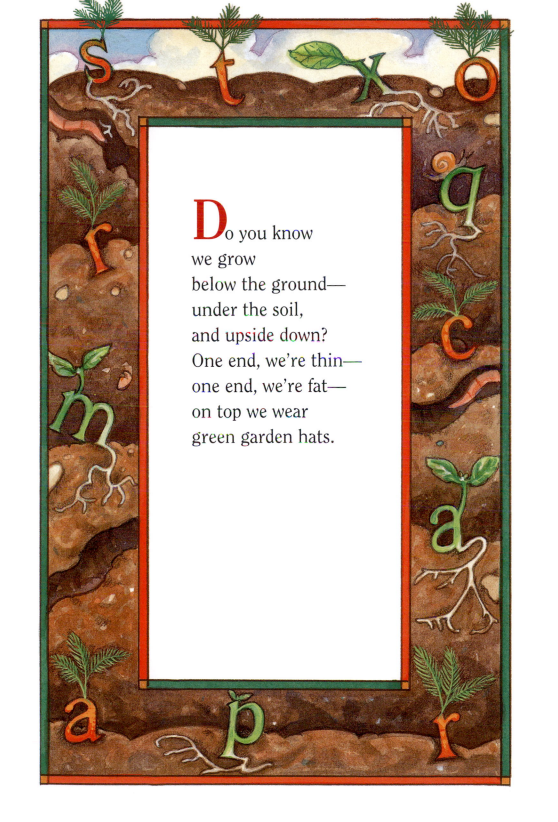

Do you know
we grow
below the ground—
under the soil,
and upside down?
One end, we're thin—
one end, we're fat—
on top we wear
green garden hats.

I'm nice and hot
and good for you.
You slurp me up,
and when you're through,
the giant hole
that I swam in
becomes
an empty
bowl again.

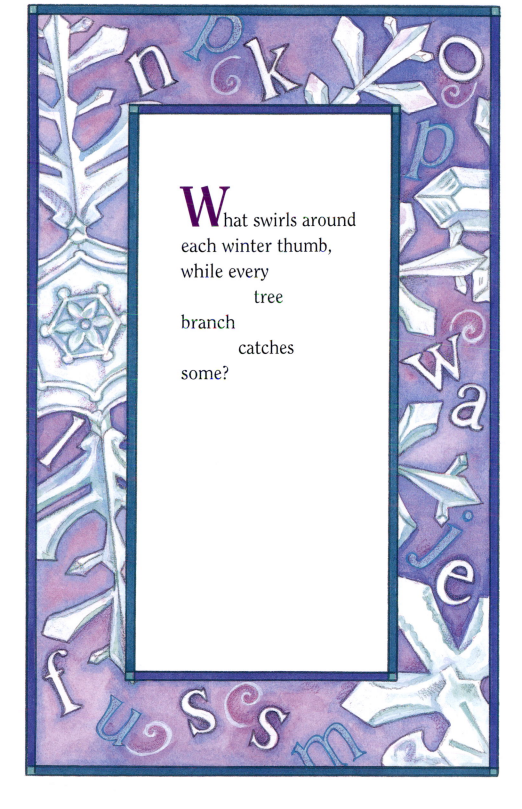

What swirls around
each winter thumb,
while every
            tree
branch
            catches
some?

Tiny globes
of colored
glass;
spinning,
rolling,
as they pass
cracks
in sidewalks,
stones
in streets—
circling,
colliding
on smooth
concrete.

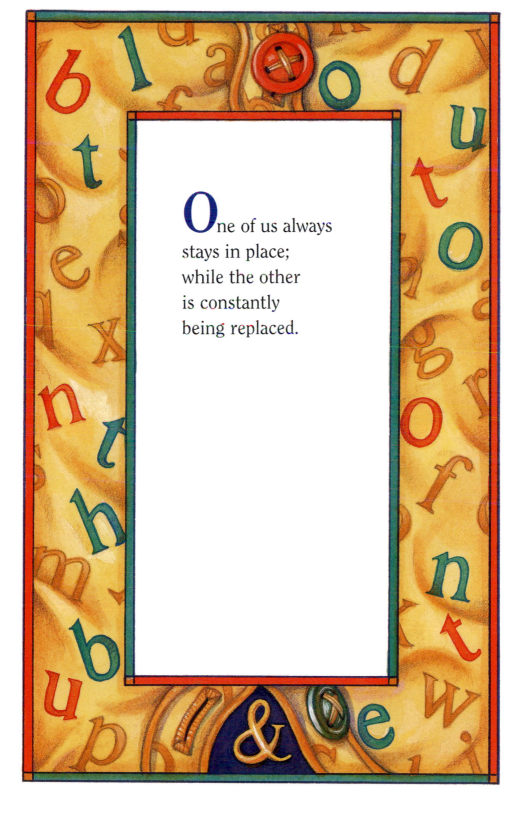

One of us always
stays in place;
while the other
is constantly
being replaced.

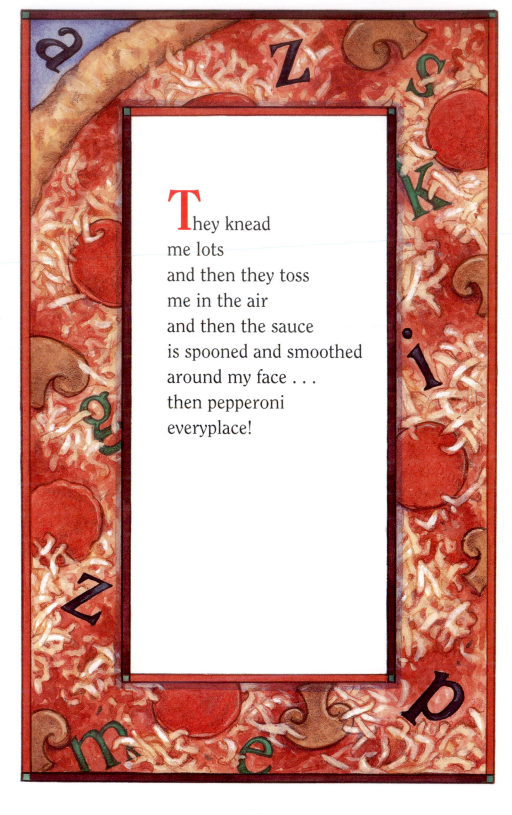

They knead
me lots
and then they toss
me in the air
and then the sauce
is spooned and smoothed
around my face . . .
then pepperoni
everyplace!

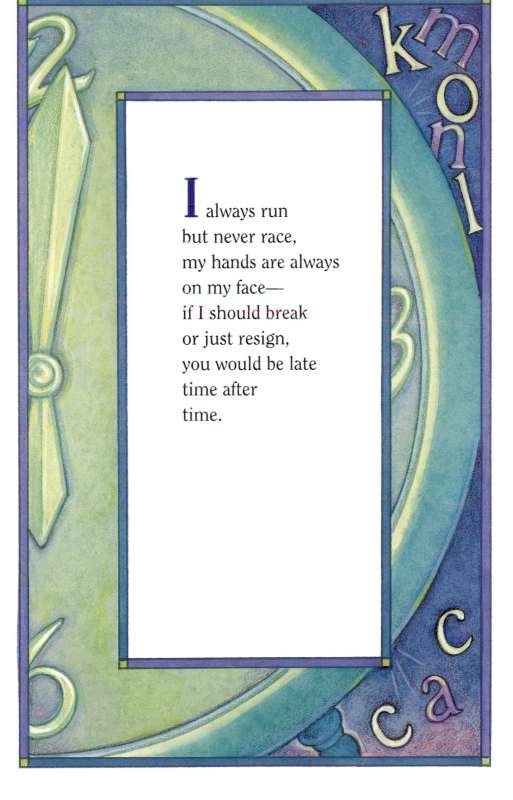

I always run
but never race,
my hands are always
on my face—
if I should break
or just resign,
you would be late
time after
time.

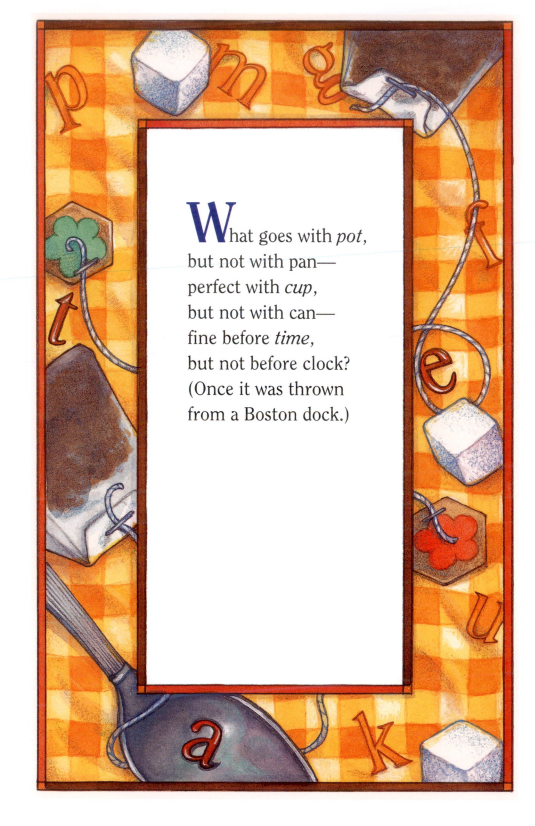

What goes with *pot*,
but not with pan—
perfect with *cup*,
but not with can—
fine before *time*,
but not before clock?
(Once it was thrown
from a Boston dock.)

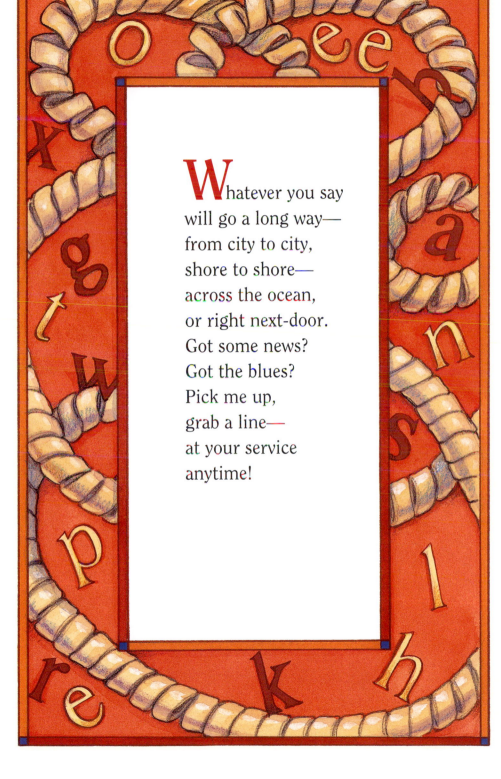

Whatever you say
will go a long way—
from city to city,
shore to shore—
across the ocean,
or right next-door.
Got some news?
Got the blues?
Pick me up,
grab a line—
at your service
anytime!

Shut me tight,
and lock the lock—
I won't tell,
and I won't talk.

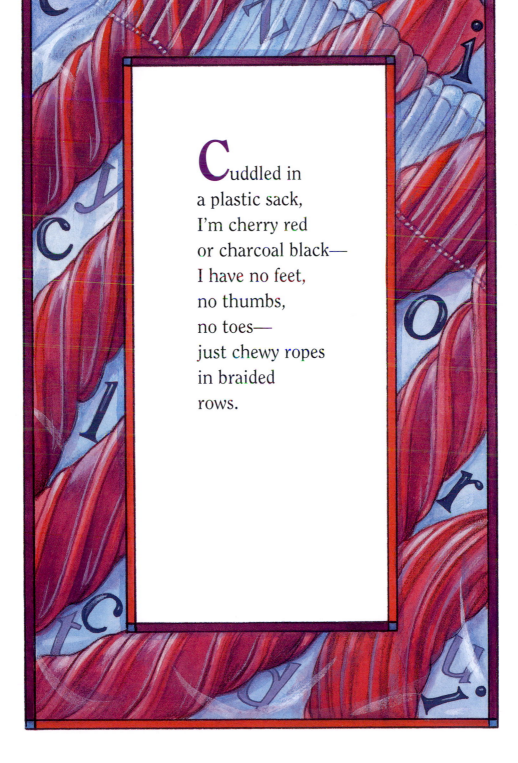

Cuddled in
a plastic sack,
I'm cherry red
or charcoal black—
I have no feet,
no thumbs,
no toes—
just chewy ropes
in braided
rows.

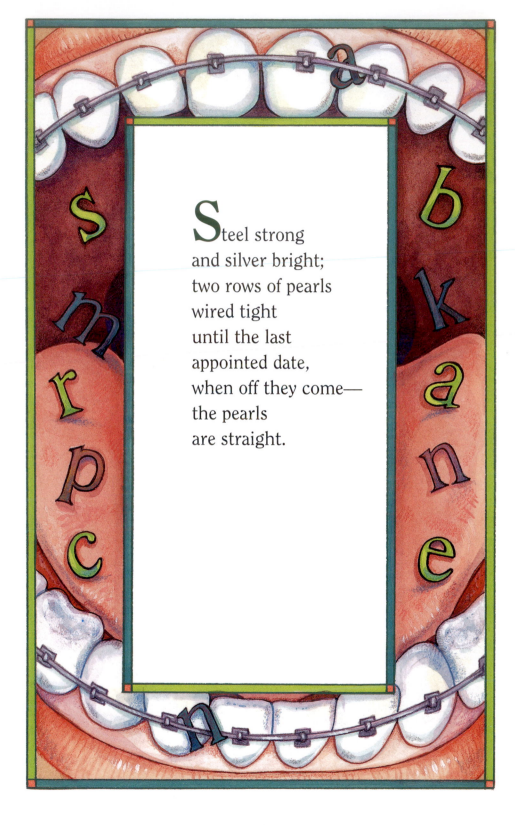

Steel strong
and silver bright;
two rows of pearls
wired tight
until the last
appointed date,
when off they come—
the pearls
are straight.

Cables are on
outriggers
          are   out
I swing my hook
and line about;
I shoot out my boom,
swivel my cab,
          pick up a pole,
a concrete slab.
The hours go by;
I work with zeal—
rigging up bales
of bundled
steel.

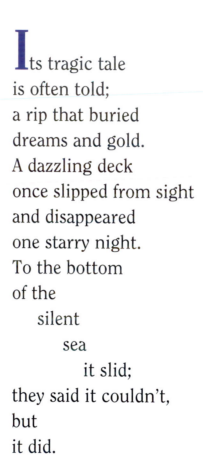

Its tragic tale
is often told;
a rip that buried
dreams and gold.
A dazzling deck
once slipped from sight
and disappeared
one starry night.
To the bottom
of the
        silent
                sea
                    it slid;
they said it couldn't,
but
it did.

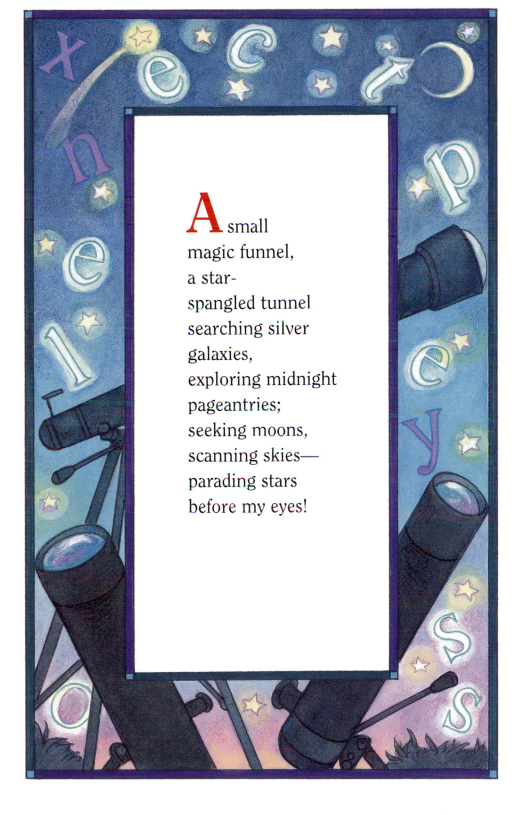

A small
magic funnel,
a star-
spangled tunnel
searching silver
galaxies,
exploring midnight
pageantries;
seeking moons,
scanning skies—
parading stars
before my eyes!

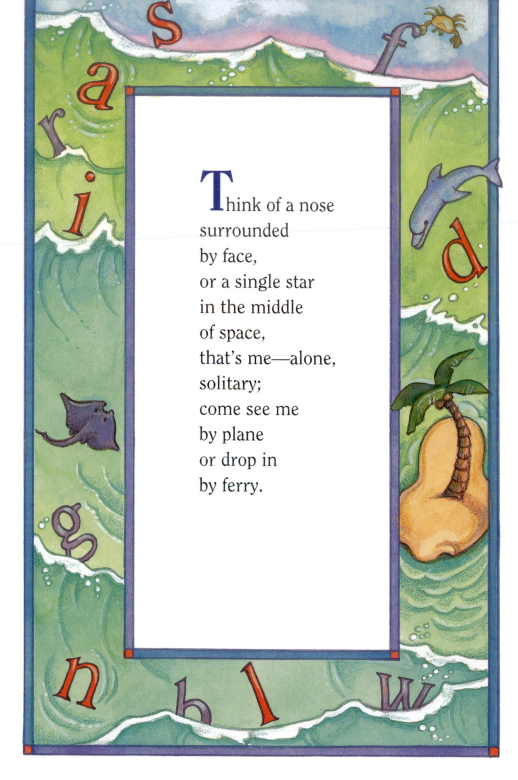

Think of a nose
surrounded
by face,
or a single star
in the middle
of space,
that's me—alone,
solitary;
come see me
by plane
or drop in
by ferry.

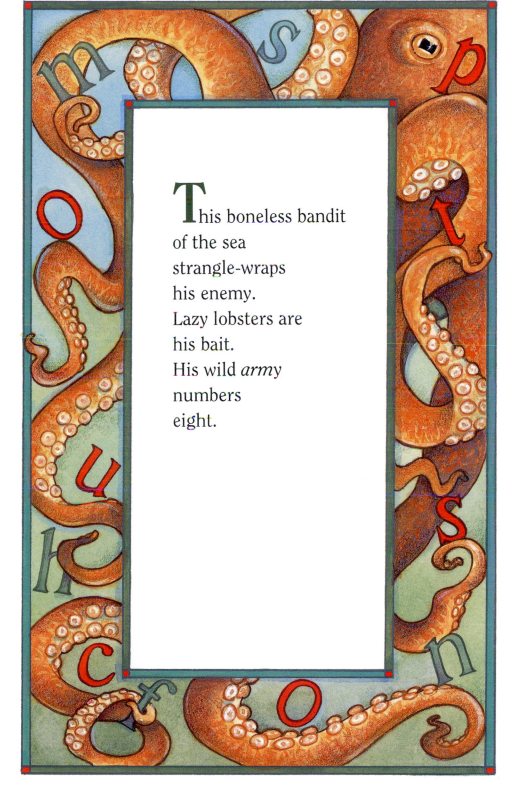

This boneless bandit
of the sea
strangle-wraps
his enemy.
Lazy lobsters are
his bait.
His wild *army*
numbers
eight.

You polish your riddles,
you rhyme,
you write—
you work to place
your words just right.
When the lines look fine
you usually know it—
can you guess who you are?
That's right, you're a ____.